Project Management Institute

D0862556

Effectiveness in Project Portfolio Management

Peerasit Patanakul, PhD
Audrey Curtis, PhD
Brian Koppel, MBA, PMP

Library of Congress Cataloging-in-Publication Data

ISBN: 978-1-935589-86-0

Published by: Project Management Institute, Inc.
                                 14 Campus Boulevard
                                 Newtown Square, Pennsylvania 19073-3299 USA
                                 Phone: +610-356-4600
                                 Fax: +610-356-4647
                                 Email: customercare@pmi.org
                                 Internet: www.PMI.org

PMI Publications welcomes corrections and comments on its books. Please feel free to send comments on typographical, formatting, or other errors. Simply make a copy of the relevant page of the book, mark the error, and send it to: Book Editor, PMI Publications, 14 Campus Boulevard, Newtown Square, PA 19073-3299 USA.

To inquire about discounts for resale or educational purposes, please contact the PMI Book Service Center.

                                 PMI Book Service Center
                                 P.O. Box 932683, Atlanta, GA 31193-2683 USA
                                 Phone: 1-866-276-4764 (within the U.S. or Canada)
                                 or +1-770-280-4129 (globally)
                                 Fax: +1-770-280-4113
                                 Email: info@bookorders.pmi.org

MIX
Paper from
responsible sources
FSC® C015782
www.fsc.org

Table of Contents

Preface

While project portfolio management (PPM) has increased its significance in various business contexts, research on effectiveness of PPM is still limited. In fact, PPM effectiveness has not been clearly defined and factors contributing to PPM effectiveness have not been thoroughly investigated. The lack of such research has practitioners continuing with a PPM approach that has not been measured as to its effectiveness and impact on business results.

This book presents the findings from a major research initiative to investigate PPM effectiveness from actual business settings in order to propose a definition of PPM effectiveness, identify factors impacting PPM effectiveness, and propose criteria for measuring such effectiveness. The findings from this research should be a foundation for future studies and provide practitioners with a guideline for creating organizational conditions that promote PPM.

Chapter 1 of the book discusses the current state of research on project portfolio management effectiveness and the literature on effectiveness. Chapter 2 presents the methodology of this research. Chapter 3 discusses the practices of PPM of the organizations in this study. Chapter 4 presents our proposed definition of PPM effectiveness. Chapter 5 discusses key factors impacting PPM effectiveness. The criteria for measuring PPM effectiveness are presented in Chapter 6. Chapter 7 concludes the research with the theoretical contribution and managerial implications of this research.

We hope that the contents in this book will serve as a foundation for future PPM research and practices.

Peerasit Patanakul

Audrey Curtis

Brian Koppel

Acknowledgments

This research was supported by the generous participation of five organizations that allowed the research team to conduct extensive interviews with key members of their organizations. While the names of these organizations must be kept confidential, they receive our gratitude for their contributions of time and frank discussions that form the substance of this book. We are especially thankful to PMI for the funding support, to our PMI Research Liaison Marge Combe and to the staff of the Academic and Research group of PMI that runs the research program.

Chapter 1

Introduction

This study was conducted to investigate PPM effectiveness in real-life business settings in order to propose a definition of PPM effectiveness, identify factors impacting PPM effectiveness, and propose criteria for measuring such effectiveness.

4/11/2013

Current Research on Project Portfolio Management Effectiveness

Project portfolio management (PPM) has been practiced in many organizations as an approach to coordinate a portfolio of projects or programs, to achieve specific organizational objectives (PMI, 2008). A typical goal of PPM is to ensure that an organization is doing the right work rather than doing the work right (PMI, 2008). From industry practices, Cooper, Edgett, & Kleinschmidt, (2001) suggest that the maximization of portfolio value, portfolio balance, and strategic alignment are the typical goals of PPM for new product development.

To accomplish PPM goals, several authors have proposed PPM frameworks, which include those for project portfolio selection (Archer & Ghasemzadeh, 1999) and management of portfolios in different settings (Kendall & Rollins, 2003; Rad & Levin, 2005; Rajegopal, McGuin, & Waller, 2007). Early research on PPM methodologies focused on R&D project/portfolio selection and evaluation (Bard, Balachandra,

& Kaufmann, 1988; Chiu & Gear, 1979; Golabi, 1987; Khorramshahgol & Gousty, 1986; Madey & Dean, 1985; Spharim & Szakonyi, 1984). This trend continues and methodologies have been developed for different settings and conditions, such as a specific decision support system to identify an optimal project portfolio mix under uncertainty for information system projects (Kira, Kusy, Murray, & Goranson, 1990), a model for optimizing interdependent projects over multiple time periods (Dickinson, Thornton, & Graves, 2001), and a model for interactive R&D portfolio analysis dealing with project interdependencies and time profiles of multiple objectives (Stummer & Heidenberger, 2003). Besides the methodologies proposed in a form of mathematical models discussed above, several authors suggested simpler methodologies for PPM that include economic/financial models such as payback period, net present value, bang for buck index, productivity index, profitability index, and expected commercial value (Cooper et al., 2001; PMI, 2006; Rajegopal et al., 2007). Scoring models were also proposed for project selection and evaluation, while bubble diagrams were suggested for portfolio balancing. Product and technology roadmaps and strategic buckets were suggested in part for strategy-portfolio alignment (Cooper et al., 2001). The stage-gate approach was also proposed for portfolio management (Cooper, Edgett, & Kleinschmidt, 2002).

While some of the PPM frameworks and methodologies, including a standard for PPM (PMI, 2008), have been widely practiced, a simple question asked by practitioners is *whether or not their PPM is effective*. In the literature, research on PPM effectiveness is still limited. Several studies were conducted on PPM efficiency and performance (Blomquist & Muller, 2006; Martinsuo & Lehtonen, 2007). Even though the understanding of PPM efficiency is beneficial, the comprehension of PPM effectiveness cannot be overlooked. The use of the proposed frameworks and methodologies may be the means for achieving PPM effectiveness; however, one will not know until PPM effectiveness is defined. The objective of this study is to investigate PPM effectiveness from a real-life business setting in order to propose a definition of PPM effectiveness, identify factors impacting PPM effectiveness, and propose criteria for measuring such effectiveness. A case-study research methodology was employed. To establish a better understanding of effectiveness in an organizational context, the literature on organizational, team, and project management effectiveness was reviewed and summarized in the following section.

Literature on Effectiveness

In the literature, effectiveness has been the center of attention of several scholars of management research. Several studies have been conducted to investigate effectiveness at the organizational and team levels. An attempt to define organizational effectiveness dates back to the "Scientific Management" approach of Frederick Taylor (1911) who perceived organizational effectiveness in terms of production maximization, technical excellence, and optimal utilization of resources. Taking the human relations' view, several researchers refer to effectiveness as productivity through employee satisfaction (Likert, 1961; Mayo, 1933; McGregor, 1960). From the strategic management and design perspective, organizational effectiveness is viewed with respect to structure/strategy congruence, competitive attainment, and environmental control and flexibility/adaptation (Chandler, 1962). Later, researchers focused on using multiple perspectives to determine organizational effectiveness. Pennings and Goodman (1977) indicated that "organizations are effective if relevant constraints can be satisfied and if organizational results approximate or exceed a set of referents for multiple goals." Later, other researchers such as Brundney and Englund (1982) and Elmes and Wilemon (1988) had similar perceptions. Building on the works of several researchers such as Scott (1977), Cameron (1979), and Seashore (1979), Quinn and Rohrbaugh (1983) proposed a "Spatial Model" of organizational effectiveness, resulting from mapping various effectiveness constructs. This Spatial Model includes three competing values (organizational focus, structure, and means and ends) and four middle-range models of organizational analysis (human relation, open system, internal process, and rational goal). Several researchers suggest that it would be generally more promising if an organization-specific model based on clear and explicit assumptions were developed (Campbell, 1977; Lewin & Minton, 1986). The organizational effectiveness would then be the degree to which the organization's "end" objectives are accomplished, subject to certain constraints. Many scholars also suggested that the nature of effectiveness is multidimensional and should be defined by a complex of stakeholders, who may in fact hold different and incompatible perspectives (Cameron & Whetten, 1983; Lewin & Minton, 1986).

In addition to organizational effectiveness, team effectiveness was of interest to many researchers and was typically studied as part of an input-process-outcome (IPO) framework (Denison, Hart, & Kahn, 1996; Mathieu, Maynard, Rapp, & Gilson, 2008; McGrath, 1964;). In the IPO framework, inputs describe antecedent factors that enable and constrain members' interaction such as individual member characteristics (e.g., skills and personalities), team characteristics (e.g., structure and managerial influences), and organizational contextual factors (e.g., environmental complexity and organizational design). Processes describe members' interactions directed toward task accomplishment. The outcomes in the IPO framework are typically the criteria of effectiveness, which are results and by-products of team activity that are valued by one or more constituencies.

The outcomes may include team performance and members' affective reactions (e.g., satisfaction). In their study of self-managing work teams, Cohen, Ledford, and Spreitzer (1996) defined effectiveness in terms of performance effectiveness (e.g., controlling costs, improving productivity, and quality), employee attitude about their quality of life (e.g., job satisfaction and organization commitment), and employee behavior. For cross-functional teams, Denison, Hart, and Kahn (1996) specifically measured the outcomes in terms of information creation, team compression, image expansion, learning, growth satisfaction, capability development, and overall effectiveness.

In project management literature, even though project management effectiveness is of interest to many researchers, few researchers have attempted to define it. With his focus on understanding the impact of effectiveness and efficiency on project success, Phelan (2004) simply refers to effectiveness as the extent of accomplishment of the right things, the right ends; and efficiency as the economics of doing things right, the economics of the right means. Without defining project management effectiveness, Morrison and Brown (2004) propose a conceptual construct of project management effectiveness, which includes multiple dimensions, namely organizational input, project management process, short-term results, and strategic impact. This conceptual construct is similar to the IPO framework of team effectiveness (Cohen & Ledford, 1994; Denison et al., 1996). The organizational inputs are a supportive organization and rational project decision making. The processes include effective tools and systems, procedures and discipline, project leadership, project communication, resource adequacy and competency, and customer-process integration. The outcomes in terms of short-term results and strategic impact are about meeting project operational objectives consistently, meeting organizational strategic goals for project management, and smoothly integrating project management into organization's workflow.

The review of the literature helped this research in many ways. The understanding of organizational, team, and project management effectiveness helps guide the development of research instruments and the development of a definition for PPM effectiveness.

Chapter 2

Research Method

Case-study research was employed as the methodology. PPM practices of five organizations, for-profit and not-for-profit, were investigated. These organizations are in the telecommunication services, insurance, insurance services, and financial services industries. A research and development center of the U.S. government is also included in this study.

Design and Sampling

With the limited knowledge and perspective on PPM effectiveness, case study was used as the methodology (Eisenhardt, 1989; Yin, 1984). PPM practices of five organizations were investigated. These organizations are leaders in their respective areas.

Alpha is a leader in telecommunications services. The company consists of several business units, one of which is the global shared-services (GSS) business group. GSS operates the company's wire line network, including providing support across business units for finance operations, real estate, and supply chain services. Within GSS, PPM of the wire line network (product development and product deployment projects) was the focus of this study.

Beta is in the insurance services industry. The company's products help customers protect life, property, and financial assets in the United States and around the world. To serve its clients, the company draws upon experience in data management and security and expertise in predictive modeling. PPM of the company's information technology organization was investigated in this study.

Delta is in the insurance industry. The company meets the needs of its clients through life insurance, disability insurance, investment management, and other financial services. The focus of this study was on the management of a portfolio of corporate projects. These projects are either strategically or operationally important to the company. Software development projects are the majority of the portfolio.

Gamma is an international financial services company. The technology group is divided into units that support the various business areas, as well as units that cut across the organization. The study covers a portfolio of technology projects that includes include both software development and infrastructure initiatives.

Lambda is a research and development center of the U.S. government. Its staff consists of over 3,000 civilian engineers, scientists, and support personnel. The focus of this study is the portfolio of emerging technology projects.

Data Collection

To investigate PPM practices, six to ten individuals from each organization were interviewed at their business locations. These individuals were representatives from various management levels, including senior-level executives such as president, executive vice president, vice president, CFO, and CIO. At the PPM and project management levels, the information was gathered from the directors of PPM, the project management office (PMO) managers, PPM committee members, and PMO personnel. Additionally, the directors of project management were interviewed to help the researchers gain an understanding of the project management practices of each organization. Interviews were also conducted with representatives from the business units. The interviews with informants from different management levels helped the researchers understand the PPM practices of that organization from different perspectives.

These semi-structured interviews typically lasted about 60 minutes, except the interviews with the PPM director of *Delta* and the director of the Project Integration Office of *Lambda*, which lasted approximately 150 minutes each. These interviews were conducted to gather information regarding the PPM processes and methodologies used in each organization, the roles and responsibilities of the informants in PPM, the informants' view of their PPM practices, the placement of PPM and project management, and the informants' view of PPM effectiveness. Depending on the roles and responsibilities of the informant, some specific questions regarding strategic planning process, capital budgeting and portfolio funding, organizational culture, resource allocation, and governance were also asked. All interviews were conducted at the informants' setting using two researchers. The interviews were also tape-recorded.

Data Analysis

Each interview was transcribed, yielding approximately 15-30 pages of transcript. The transcripts were coded and the chains of evidence were developed. For each organization, within-case analysis was conducted. The documents received from the respondents (e.g., PPM processes, scoring sheets, and project prioritization documents) were reviewed. Cross-case analysis was also conducted to analyze the consistency and inconsistency of the data across cases and to ensure the construct and internal validity of the findings (Eisenhardt, 1989; Miles & Huberman,

1980; Yin, 1984). After these analyses, the findings were compared and contrasted with the literature on organizational and team effectiveness to identify the similarity/dissimilarity and for the external validation.

In terms of the research results, a definition of PPM effectiveness was developed as a result of the cross-case analysis and literature review. After the development of the definition, each case was revisited to investigate whether the case data confirmed the definition of PPM effectiveness. The cross-case analysis also helps us identify key factors impacting PPM effectiveness and potential criteria for measuring PPM effectiveness. The research results are presented in the next chapters.

Chapter 3

Project Portfolio Management in Practices

The five organizations use different approaches to PPM. While some organizations have an independent entity for PPM, the others manage their portfolio as part of their business operations. Despite their different approaches, these organizations practice portfolio alignment and portfolio monitoring and control processes. Senior-level executives of these organizations are involved in the portfolio governance. All five organizations practice standardized project management processes and methodologies.

PPM Practices in Each Organization

Alpha is a communications services company serving the U.S. market with communications services for residential and business customers. In this study, we investigated the portfolio of network projects, which is managed under a network program management office (Network PMO) of the global shared-services (GSS) business group. The purpose of the Network PMO is to ensure the delivery of the network projects. In general, the project funding process starts with a capital planning process at the corporate level. Each business unit (BU) enters its initiatives as part of a capital request in the company's capital planning tool. After the investigation of the ROI at the corporate level and at each BU level, including the deliberated discussions and negotiations, funds are allocated to each BU.

In the network portfolio of GSS, the network projects are typically originated from marketing initiatives. During the preparation of a project for the selection and prioritization process, there are project sizing and costing activities that require collaboration between marketing and the network PMO. Based on the availability of funds, the executive committee (with support from marketing) selects projects based on projected revenue generation. The priority of the projects depends on the business priority and is set by the marketing team. The marketing team maintains a list of funded projects to be rolled out in a given year, including their priority, and makes the list available to the Network PMO. After being funded, the projects are planned and executed by the Network PMO.

As for project management, the Network PMO has a project management system that includes standardized project management processes and methodologies. The standard project management practices are followed depending on the type of project and there is information systems support to help with recording and reporting status and progress. During project execution, besides regular project status meetings, there is a monthly meeting to review the status of key projects with senior executives. The president and executives of GSS pay particular attention to the projects with the highest potential business impact and typically request a quarterly meeting with the project teams. Overall, *Alpha* has a mature strategic planning process. Through the executive committee, the project selection process, and the project governance by senior executives, the network portfolio had linkage to the overall business strategy.

Beta is an information services company serving the global insurance industry with statistical, actuarial, and claims-related products. At *Beta*, the project portfolio is managed under the project management office of the development division (Development PMO), established three-to-five years ago. The development division is aligned with businesses, having a manager and necessary resources for each unit. While there is no designated PPM office and staff, the Development PMO serves in this role. The portfolio consists of multiple development and infrastructure projects within the IT organization. The purpose of the PMO is to ensure the smooth utilization of resources, to alleviate resource contention issues, and to successfully manage high-priority projects in the portfolio. The PMO has a full-time PMO manager and seven project managers (direct reports). Other project managers reside within infrastructure and development organizations (indirect reports to the PMO manager). At any given time, there are approximately 30-40 projects in the portfolio.

Projects are typically initiated by the business during a budget cycle or an off cycle. Product managers (from the business units) and the PMO manager work collaboratively to develop requirements documents and the project charter. The project selection is conducted at the cross-business executive level. Major projects require approval from the CEO. This is accomplished annually as part of the capital budgeting process, providing funding for business operations. Once approved, the projects are listed in the portfolio dashboard and categorized and scored by the PMO manager. The project ranking is performed by the prioritization committee (BPC), consisting of four senior executives from the IT department. The rank of the project determines its priority when there is resource contention. The top 10 projects typically receive all the resources they need. The company has introduced tools and procedures that promote consistency in how the portfolio is prioritized and managed. For example, the PMO utilizes scoring sheets and systems to manage the ranking from the score sheets from each rater.

Projects follow a toll gate process for project management, once approved. An online system was implemented and is used on a daily basis to ensure visibility into the projects and for tracking project status and issues. The system is available to all and supports transparency across the business and with management, according to the established hierarchy of permissions. There is an automatic notification if there are any conflicts or issues. The process is regarded as providing substantial improvement and benefit to the business. The PMO manager has a weekly meeting with project managers to discuss resource conflicts in the upcoming weeks. Another weekly meeting is also set to go over dashboard, milestones, and processes. *Beta* follows a strategic planning process. IT strategy was developed using top-down and bottom-up approaches. A strategic exercise is used to develop 10, 7, 3, and next-year visions and goals. These visions and goals are used as a foundation for the development of quarterly objectives and metrics.

Delta is an insurance company that has a dedicated corporate level project portfolio management office (PPMO), reporting to the vice president of strategy. The office has a dedicated director and staff. The PPMO is directly involved with the selection, prioritization, and governance of the corporate project portfolio through a prioritization committee (PC) and a project review committee (RC). The majority of approximately 40 projects in the portfolio were IT-related projects.

The PC is chaired by the director of the PPMO. The committee members are senior-level managers representing various functions, including businesses. The company's senior executives are not involved in making funding decisions, but they provide their perspective on the priority of projects related to the strategic direction of the company. *Delta* also has a benefit realization team (BT). This team is a result of a recent initiative to measure the realization of benefits from projects.

The BT helps project teams identify benefits of their projects prior to presenting project proposals to the PC. The PC has sole authority in making project funding decisions and reports directly to the management committee, which consists of the company's senior executives. The PPMO maintains active oversight of the portfolio of projects through the RC, chaired by the director of PPMO. The RC emphasizes project delivery and provides inputs to the PC to make the go/kill decisions. For each project, funding decisions are made on a phase-by-phase basis. The quality process consultants, part of the IT excellence and quality organization, provide assistance to project managers to ensure project delivery. All corporate projects follow a standardized project management process that incorporates the interactions with the PC, RC, and BT. *Delta* has a mature strategic planning process. The organization has a company strategy map, including drivers and metrics. While the company's strategy does not change very often, it is revisited every 12-18 months and reviewed regularly.

Gamma is an international finance company that has a large portion of its projects involved with systems that support the firm's various financial transactions. The company has a dedicated PMO team that is part of the technology organization and reports into the CIO. The PMO is primarily concerned with project governance and facilitates monthly meetings with the CIO and the senior IT management team to review project status. Each project that meets the minimum criteria, as defined by the project steering committee, is reviewed on a monthly basis through a project summary report that is prepared by the project team. The PMO also manages compliance to the company's project life cycle and standardized documentation requirements, which is tracked via an online tool that can provide metrics and reporting around adherence to the processes.

The project portfolio is managed by a steering committee that consists of corporate-level executives, representatives of the various business units with the technology managers that directly support them, and members of the finance department. During the fourth quarter of each year, each business unit and its technology counterparts identify the large projects that seek to be initiated in the following year. A capital sheet template is completed for each of these proposed projects and includes project cost and benefit information. After the list of potential projects is reduced through preliminary discussions, it is presented to the steering committee, and a subset of the requests receives approval for funding in the following year. This selection committee meets on a quarterly basis to review the entire portfolio and make decisions as to whether the current set of projects should proceed or if there are any projects that need to cease. New "unplanned" projects may also request funding at these quarterly meetings.

After projects receive funding approval from the portfolio steering committee, there is a high-level planning meeting held with the CIO and the technology management team. This meeting provides visibility to the management team into upcoming projects that may require their resources. Also, those projects that receive approval to proceed are authorized to spend a subset of the funds granted for initial analysis. The next step is a review of the planned architecture to ensure it is consistent with corporate standards and that there is no redundancy. Once the project is ready to move to the next stage, it goes through one last review, led by the CIO and CFO, for authorization to spend the budgeted dollars. The project is then subject to the monthly project status review.

Lambda is a research and development center of the U.S. government. The organization is comprised of a large number of units, including engineering centers and enterprise offices.

As a governmental center, *Lambda* receives funds from different sources, resulting in different categories of projects and different portfolios. The portfolio of emerging technology projects (ETP) was the focus of this study. There are approximately 40-50 projects in the portfolio. The ETP portfolio is championed by the director of science concept and technology (SC&T), who is a visionary and has a broad understanding of dependencies among technologies, including *Lambda*'s strategy and war fighters' interests. Without a dedicated office, the SC&T director is supported by staff from the business interface office and the project integration office.

The annual selection and evaluation of the ETP portfolio starts from requests for proposals. The proposals are then reviewed by the quality management board (QMB), consisting of representatives from engineering centers and enterprise offices. By keeping the strategy in mind, QMB evaluates proposals against the war fighter gaps, which has priority. This process is iterative, with extensive discussions between QMB and the proposal owner. After the evaluation, QMB proposes a list of projects to the SC&T director, who then makes the final selection. After funding, the projects are executed with the assistance of a project integrator (PI), who will contact the proposal owner and initiate the selection of a project manager. After the development of project preliminary documents (e.g., charter, preliminary plan, and acquisition strategy), the project funding is released by the SC&T director. The level of project (according to the category from the government) is decided and the project manager and the PI work on project execution. Project governance depends on the level of project.

Although *Lambda*'s PPM process is more ad-hoc, it has standardized project management processes. The project integration office (PIO) owns the processes and facilitates the exercise of the processes and procedures through the PIs, who directly provide assistance to project managers. The PIO has 10 PIs and assistant PIs, dedicated to different programs. The PIO also provides project management training. Additionally, the PIO facilitates project performance reviews, which are conducted at different levels of rigor, depending on the level of project. Financial reviews are conducted through a fiscal-year budgeting process.

Similarities and Differences in PPM Practices

From the analysis, these five organizations used different approaches to PPM (see Table 1). While *Delta* has an independent entity and the most mature process for PPM, the others managed their portfolio as part of their business operations with the utilization of the project management office. At the corporate level, all four for-profit organizations followed their capital budgeting process to allocate funds across businesses. As a government center, *Lambda* receives different categories of funds from the government that they have to utilize within the scope of the prescribed execution policy.

For *Alpha*'s network project portfolio, the project selection and prioritization were done by the businesses as part of the usual business operations. For *Beta*'s development project portfolio, the project selection was performed by businesses, while the prioritization was done by the IT organization to ensure the appropriate allocation of IT resources. For *Gamma,* the technology projects were proposed by each business unit and its technology counterpart. After the initial vetting process, the projects were selected by a selection committee. Different from the other companies, *Delta* allocated a discretionary budget to its corporate project portfolio and utilized an independent portfolio prioritization committee, operating separately from the company's business units. In *Lambda*'s case, the center receives funding for its ETP portfolio. The center utilizes a committee

Table 1: Similarities and differences among cases.

	Alpha	Beta	Delta	Gamma	Lambda
PPM description-unit of analysis	Network portfolio: Management of multiple network projects and program within network organization. Selection is done at the executive level	IS portfolio: Management of multiple development and infrastructure project within IS organization. Selection is done at the executive level	Corporate portfolio: Selection, prioritization, and governance of corporate portfolio.	Technology portfolio: Selection, prioritization, and management of technology portfolio	Emerging technology project (ETP) portfolio: Selection, prioritization, and governance of ETP portfolio
Funding	Part of capital budgeting process: Funding for business operations	Part of capital budgeting process: Funding for business operations	Part of capital budgeting process: Annual budget was allocated specifically for corporate portfolio	Part of capital budgeting process: Funding for business operations	Part of fiscal year funding process: Funds were allocated to different types of portfolios

(continued)

Table 1: *Continued*

	Alpha	Beta	Delta	Gamma	Lambda
PPM office/ staff	No designated PPM office and staff. Have corporate PMO for collecting information to support executive committee	No designated PPM office and staff	Designated PPM office with full-time director and staff	Office of the CIO working in cooperation with Technology PMO	Full-time SC&T director working in cooperation with designated staff from Project integration office and business interface office
Project Management Office	PMO of network organization: Management of multiple network projects and program within network organization	PMO of development organization: Management of major development and infrastructure projects	PMOs are part of IS organization, including quality process consultant	PMO of technology organization: Establish standard and provide information for PPM	Project Integration Office (PIO): Own PM and governance processes. Project integrators support project managers

(continued)

Table 1: *Continued*

	Alpha	Beta	Delta	Gamma	Lambda
Relationship with businesses	PMO provide corporate marketing with project cost and duration estimation. After selection, corporate marketing provides list of projects including priority and funding. PMO manage those projects	Project sponsors and product manager come from businesses. PMO manager works with businesses to develop requirement document and charter. Development organization is aligned with businesses	Project sponsors are from business, business representatives in the prioritization committee (PC) and project review committee (RC). Business project manager (outcome manager) has close relationship with IT project manager. Has PMO for each business	Technology organization is aligned with businesses and has relationship managers to support businesses. Each relationship manager manages his/her own project management staff	Respond to the needs of the war fighters, strategy, and competency

(continued)

Table 1: *Continued*

	Alpha	Beta	Delta	Gamma	Lambda
Selection/ Prioritization committee	Executive committee: Marketing team comes up with products or initiatives	Executive committee: Projects are initiated by businesses, and go through a toll gate process. Big projects need approval from the CEO.	Prioritization committee: Senior-level managers, chaired by portfolio manager.	Steering committee: Follow steps in technology development and delivery process.	Quality management board (QMB) rates, scores, and prioritizes proposals, SC&T director makes final decision
Portfolio Governance	PMO and executive meeting	Executive meeting	Project review committee (RC), benefit realization team (BT), PC, management committee	Monthly review for each individual project and quarterly portfolio review	Performance review depends on type of projects. Financial review through fiscal year budgeting

(continued)

Table 1: *Continued*

	Alpha	Beta	Delta	Gamma	Lambda
Project management	Follow standard project management process with the use of information systems	Follow standard project management process with the use of information systems	Follow standard project management process with the use of information systems	Follow standard project management process with the use of information systems	Follow standard project management process with the use of information systems
Involvement of senior executives	President and executives pay attention to projects that have the highest business impact	CIO leads prioritization committee	PC direct report to management committee. Support from portfolio governance team	CIO and senior executives participate in quarterly portfolio review. CIO chairs other committees	Depends on the category of project and type of funding

to evaluate the proposals. No matter what approaches the companies used, projects in their portfolio were selected to support the organization's strategic directions and operations. Since revenue generation was important for *Alpha*, the projects were selected based on the revenue they were expected to generate. *Beta*'s portfolio also supported its businesses. *Delta* utilized a benefit realization committee to unsure that the project benefits were articulated. The projects were selected and prioritized based on their benefits and their alignment with the company's strategic direction. *Gamma* emphasizes return on investment, operational improvement, and regulatory compliance during project selection. *Lambda* puts more attention to war fighters' gaps during the selection process.

As for project management, all five organizations practice standardized project management processes and methodologies. They utilize project management offices to help ensure the successful delivery of the projects in the portfolio. For *Alpha*, based on the types of products or services generated by projects, the network projects were assigned to the relevant group under the network PMO. Each group had its own project managers who were the direct reports of the group director. *Beta* utilized a centralized development PMO for managing development projects. Project managers are the direct reports of the PMO manager. Since *Delta*'s corporate projects involve IT elements, the projects were managed under the IT organization in which the IT excellence and quality group provided project management consultants to project managers to ensure successful project delivery. *Gamma* has an enterprise PMO to promote standardized project management processes and facilitate project management governance. It also has divisional PMOs that support its businesses. *Lambda* utilizes a project integration office to promote standardized project management processes and to provide assistance to the project managers.

In all five organizations, senior-level executives were involved in the portfolio governance. *Alpha*'s executives paid significant attention on the network portfolio, especially the strategic initiatives. *Beta*'s CIO and vice presidents were informed about the status of projects in the portfolio through its PMO. *Delta*'s executives received the status of the portfolio through the director of the corporate project portfolio, on behalf of the portfolio prioritization committee. *Gamma*'s CIO and senior executives are members of the portfolio steering committee. *Lambda*'s senior personnel participate in proposal selection and project governance.

Despite their different approaches to PPM, all five organizations practiced portfolio alignment and portfolio monitoring and control processes. To different degrees, these organizations employed well-defined procedures, including formal and explicit methods for project portfolio management. Even though these organizations did not employ a specific measurement to assess the portfolio success, they emphasized the success of an individual project in the portfolio. Middle managers, such as portfolio managers and PMO managers, also play major roles in PPM. All five organizations continuously learn and implement new practices to improve their PPM.

Chapter 4

A Definition of Project Portfolio Management Effectiveness

PPM effectiveness is the organizational capability to (1) form and govern a project portfolio such that the portfolio aligns with the organization's strategic direction, addresses risks and opportunities, and is adaptive to internal and external changes in order to provides short and long-term value or benefits to the organization, and (2) to manage projects in the portfolio to promote transparency, process consistency, visibility, and predictability of projects in the portfolio, and to promote integrity, cohesion, and the morale of the project community.

PPM Effectiveness in the Context of Each Organization

The research evidence indicates that, to a certain extent, PPM has been practiced in five organizations we studied, but none of them explicitly defines effectiveness in project portfolio management. With the relevant information that we have collected from the cases, we propose definitions of PPM effectiveness. First, we propose the definitions in each organization's context. Next, we define PPM effectiveness from research evidence across the cases and relevant literature.

In the case of *Alpha*, without a designated PPM office, the project portfolio is managed as an integral part of day-to-day business operations. Major projects are viewed as strategic investments. Network projects are managed by the Network PMO. The PMO provides relevant project information to executives for making portfolio decisions. Senior executives put much emphasis on balancing and managing risks of the portfolio and on the alignment of the projects in the portfolio with the organization's strategic objectives by tracking and measuring projects and the portfolio against the objectives, measured in terms of revenue. Senior executives also rely heavily on the effective management of projects in the portfolio. In *Alpha*'s context, effectiveness in project portfolio management can be defined as *the organizational capability to select and govern projects in the portfolio such that the portfolio is balanced in terms of risk and return and aligned with the organization's strategic objectives to generate financial benefits to the organization.* This definition is in line with portfolio aligning and monitoring and controlling process groups (PMI, 2008). At the Network PMO level, effectiveness in project portfolio management can be defined as *the organizational capability to manage, monitor, and control projects in the portfolio for successful project delivery, and to provide necessary information for making portfolio decisions.* In the Network PMO's context, PPM effectiveness is defined as part of portfolio execution and reporting (PMI, 2008).

In the case of *Beta*, a portfolio of development projects is managed by the Development PMO. Without the responsibility of project selection and evaluation, the PMO emphasizes successful project delivery. In particular, the PMO manager places more attention on resource utilization and conflict. The PMO utilizes information systems to promote visibility of project status, transparency of resource allocation, and communication. The CIO and VPs are informed of the status of projects in the portfolio through its Development PMO. In *Beta*'s context, the effectiveness in managing the development portfolio can be defined as *the organizational capability to manage and govern projects in the portfolio to promote successful project delivery for organizational value and benefits.* In the development portfolio context, PPM effectiveness is defined as part of portfolio alignment (project prioritization), monitoring and controlling (review and report performance), and execution and reporting (PMI, 2008).

While *Delta* has not defined PPM effectiveness, through the PPMO, *Delta* focuses on transparent project portfolio planning linked to the business strategy. *Delta* has designated committees that have full responsibility for strategic planning, portfolio alignment, and monitoring and controlling. Project execution and reporting are the responsibility of the PMO, operated under the IT organization. In addition, the committees and processes are implemented to (1) promote transparency in a decision-making approach that can promote integrity, cohesion, and the morale of the project management community; (2) adaptability to internal changes and external opportunities; and (3) control and predictability of project delivery, leading to portfolio success. In *Delta*'s context, effectiveness in project portfolio management can be defined as *the organizational capability to transparently plan and govern the project portfolio in alignment with the company's strategy and the dynamics of business conditions to generate short and long-term value and benefits to the organization and satisfaction of project management community.* As *Delta* is the most mature in PPM, its PPM effectiveness is defined with the focus on portfolio alignment and monitoring and controlling. At the PMO level, effectiveness in project portfolio management can be defined as *the organizational capability to manage, monitor, and control projects in the portfolio for successful project delivery and to provide necessary information for making portfolio decisions.* In the PMO's context, PPM effectiveness is defined as part of portfolio execution and reporting (PMI 2008).

In *Gamma*'s case, the organization follows its technology development and delivery process. This process helps create transparency and visibility of project/portfolio selection and governance. The process also helps ensure that projects support the strategic priority of the organization in terms of return on investment, operational improvement, and regulatory compliance. In *Gamma*'s context, effectiveness in project portfolio management can be defined as *the organizational capability to select and govern the projects in the portfolio such that projects are aligned with corporate strategy and the intent to initiate approved projects are clearly communicated to and approved by management to proceed under the current corporate conditions.* This definition is in line with portfolio aligning and monitoring and controlling process groups (PMI, 2008). With the standardized project management processes and the responsible functional PMO, *Gamma* also emphasizes the *management, monitoring, and controlling projects in the portfolio for successful project delivery and to provide necessary information for making portfolio decisions.* This should be considered as part of PPM effectiveness in terms of portfolio execution and reporting (PMI, 2008).

As a government entity, *Lambda* has to follow strict governmental policies and procedures on how to spend its budgets. *Lambda*'s senior personnel emphasize the selection of projects to the portfolio such that the projects address *Lambda*'s strategy and the needs of the war fighters. The senior personnel also emphasize the ability to transfer these new technologies to operations. *Lambda* has rigorous project management and governance processes. The project integration office provides project management assistance and creates project management competencies for *Lambda*. In *Lambda*'s case, effectiveness in project portfolio management can be defined as *the organizational capability to select and govern a project portfolio that addresses the organization's strategy and the needs of the war fighters. Lambda* also emphasizes the *successful project delivery through the visibility and the utilization of an enterprise project management and governance system.*

Toward a Definition of PPM Effectiveness

The different definitions of PPM effectiveness, which we defined for each organization based on the case evidence, reflect the different levels of PPM practices in these organizations and represent different PPM process groups suggested by the Project Management Institute (PMI, 2008). To achieve the overall effectiveness of PPM, the management of every process group and component process must be effective. This includes the aligning and monitoring and controlling process groups, and project execution and reporting processes. Based on cross-case analysis, we propose a definition of PPM effectiveness as:

> *"The organizational capability to (1) form and govern a project portfolio such that the portfolio aligns with the organization's strategic direction, addresses risks and opportunities, and is adaptive to the internal and external changes in order to provide short and long-term value or benefits to the organization, and (2) the ability to manage projects in the portfolio to promote transparency, process consistency, visibility and predictability of projects in the portfolio, and to promote integrity, cohesion, and the morale of the project community."*

The effectiveness in PPM, as defined above, represents the effectiveness in the selection and prioritization, resource allocation, monitoring, and control of the project portfolio such that (1) the portfolio provides values or benefits supporting an organization's strategic direction; (2) the portfolio addresses risks and opportunities; (3) the financial and physical resources are transparently allocated; (4) the relevant information is available for making decisions; (5) the portfolio is adaptive to the internal and external changes in a business environment; and (6) the project management community of the organization possesses high integrity, cohesion, and morale. This definition of PPM effectiveness was defined based on the attainment of the portfolio management outcomes, which is similar to what Pennings and Goodman (1977) suggested regarding the definition of effectiveness.

PPM Effectiveness and Maturity of PPM Practice

This definition of PPM effectiveness also suggests a different level of effectiveness, depending on the maturity of the project portfolio management practices of an organization. At the low end of the maturity level, PPM effectiveness can be defined in terms of *the organizational capability to manage projects in the portfolio to promote transparency, process consistency, visibility and predictability of projects in the portfolio, and to promote integrity, cohesion, and morale of the project community."* Some may refer to this as effectiveness in multiple project management. At the high end of maturity level, the PPM effectiveness also includes *"The organizational capability to form and govern a project portfolio such that the portfolio aligns with organization's strategic direction, addresses risks and opportunities, and is adaptive to the internal and external changes in order to provide short and long-term value or benefits to the organization."* Note that the low or high end of maturity level does not imply bad or good project portfolio management. An organization may make a conscious decision to pursue PPM effectiveness at the low end if it serves its context and purposes. This implies that the definition of PPM effectiveness gives an organization some alternatives to justify their PPM effectiveness depending on the purpose and the context of their PPM. In addition, this definition of PPM effectiveness addresses the effectiveness from the organizational perspective and from the perspective of the project management community. It, therefore, supports the notion that effectiveness is a multi-dimensional concept. It also reflects different models of organizational effectiveness suggested in the literature (Cameron, 1979; Scott, 1977; Seashore, 1979).

Chapter 5

What Impacts Project Portfolio Management Effectiveness?

To achieve PPM effectiveness, an organization must create conditions to promote it. The results from this case study research suggest that those conditions are, but not limited to, formal strategic planning and capital budgeting, organizational entities responsible for project and portfolio management and their placement, frameworks and processes for project portfolio management and information systems support, organizational culture, and committed, active, and competent participants.

Formal Strategic Planning

As PPM effectiveness is defined as an organizational capability to form and govern a project portfolio such that the portfolio aligns with the organization's strategic direction, having a clear and articulated strategy is therefore important to effective PPM. With a clear and articulated strategy, projects can be selected to support the strategy. This also includes the deployment of strategy to objectives and metrics for strategy execution. We found research evidence that the organizations in our study practice formal strategic planning, including capital budgeting for strategy formulation and execution.

In the case of *Alpha,* the company develops a five-year strategic plan based on market competition, economic indicators, and past performance. This five-year plan is used to develop a strategic plan for each year. *Alpha*'s projects are selected to reflect the strategic plan. During execution, projects are tracked and measured against the strategy, especially the revenue impacted by project performance. Similar processes are found in company *Beta,* where management utilizes formal strategic planning to develop the business strategy. IT strategy is developed using a top-down and bottom-up approach. Management follows a strategic exercise to develop multi-year strategy views, including visions and goals. These visions and goals are used as a foundation for the development of quarterly objectives and metrics. This information is used for project prioritization such that the PMO manager can allocate project resources effectively.

In *Delta*'s case, the company utilizes a formal strategic planning process to develop a three-year strategic plan. The strategies are deployed to all levels of the organization through strategy maps, which include capabilities, drivers, and outcomes. The strategy map drives the behavior of individuals within the organization to be more strategy-focused. Projects are selected to support these strategies. *Gamma* also practices strategic planning. Various initiatives are undertaken to address the company's strategy. As a government center, *Lambda* practices strategic planning even though it may not be as mature as the other organizations. The organization has the lists of strategic areas and competencies that they need to develop. These lists drive project selection to various portfolios. In terms of budget allocation, all four for-profit companies practice formal capital budgeting in order to allocate funds for strategy execution. In the cases of *Alpha, Beta,* and *Gamma,* funds are allocated to the businesses and corporate functions, which can be used for operations and projects. For *Delta,* discretionary funds are allocated separately for the corporate projects portfolio, managed by the PPMO. *Lambda* practices fiscal-year budgeting. Budgets are allocated to *Lambda* with the execution policy from the government.

Organizational Entities Responsible for Project and Portfolio Management and Their Organizational Placement

It is evident that all organizations in this study have the organizational entities that are responsible for project management and, to a certain extent, portfolio management. Although each is named differently, each organization has a project management office (PMO) that is responsible for successful project delivery. This means that besides the responsibilities of the PMO in terms of creating standards and procedures and promoting their use, the PMO has full responsibility in managing the projects and resides in the organizational functions where the projects are executed. To a certain extent, in all five cases, the PMOs have a full-time PMO manager who has project managers as direct reports.

Led by a senior-level executive, the Network PMO of *Alpha* has four directors who have project managers as direct reports. These four directorates are arranged based on the category of network projects. In company *Beta*, the Development PMO, residing in a technology division, is responsible for managing strategically important development and infrastructure projects and for creating consistency in the use of project management processes. The full-time PMO manager is also responsible for managing resources across projects to eliminate resource conflict and to ensure the proper utilization of resources. Company *Delta* also has PMOs which operate as part of the technology organization. For *Delta*, a PMO supports each business unit and/ or corporate function of the company. *Delta* also implements a quality office (QO), which provides coaching and mentoring to project managers. The QO is responsible for the consistent use of project management processes and for project governance. The QO provides project status information to the other PPM committees. In addition to an enterprise PMO, which is responsible for the establishment of standardized project management processes and methodologies, *Gamma* utilizes division PMOs to ensure successful project delivery. *Gamma*'s functional PMOs are aligned with each of the business units and are the home bases for project managers who will lead projects for each business. Gamma also utilizes an Enterprise PMO, which is responsible for establishing standard processes and methodologies for project management across the organization. For *Lambda*, a Project Integration Office (PIO) is an enterprise unit that sets and owns project management and governance processes. Although *Lambda*'s project managers do not reside in the PIO, the office consists of project integrators who provide project management guidance and assistance to the project managers. The PIO also provides project management training.

In addition to a PMO, an organization with a high degree of PPM maturity implements a PPM office (PPMO) to promote effectiveness in project portfolio management. In *Delta*'s case, a PPMO, operating under the corporate planning division (CPD), is a designated entity for project portfolio management. It is a conscious decision that the PPMO resides under the CPD. By doing so, the PPMO is placed close to the functions responsible for strategic planning activities. The PPMO is also isolated from the influence of the business units such that it can function as a less political and less parochial unit. The PPMO has a full-time director and staff. The responsibility of the PPMO is to establish and ensure the consistent utilization of standards and procedures for PPM. The director of the PPMO chairs the project selection and prioritization committee (PC) and the project review committee (RC). As part of the PPMO's responsibility, the PPMO director communicates the portfolio status to senior executives.

Frameworks and Processes for Project Portfolio Management and Information Systems Support

Consistently using frameworks and processes for project portfolio management helps promote PPM effectiveness. In particular, they help promote transparency, consistency, visibility, and predictability in PPM. This includes frameworks and processes for project selection and prioritization, project governance, and project management. The use of frameworks and processes is evident in all organizations in this study. Depending on the degree of PPM maturity, different frameworks and processes are used in these organizations, as described below.

All five organizations practice standard project management and governance processes with gate reviews, formal documentation, and formal approval. These processes are tailored to different types of projects and mainly used to ensure successful project delivery. All organizations utilize information systems to keep records of project documentation and to facilitate information sharing with the stakeholders. As the most mature PPM, *Delta* utilizes a specific framework that includes processes, tools and techniques, and deliverables for project portfolio management and portfolio governance. *Delta*'s framework also includes the roles and responsibilities of the organization's bodies associated with PPM such as the prioritization committee, project review committee, and management committee. The framework also incorporates the interaction of these committees with the other committees within the organization, such as the interaction between the gate review committee and the quality office. In *Gamma*'s case, the organization implements its technology development and delivery process that strategic projects have to utilize. The process starts from a broad investment review to more detailed architecture and financial reviews. Senior executives take part in this process as chairs and members of various committees. This finding supports previous research, which suggests that as the level of PPM maturity increases, organizations tend to have higher degrees of portfolio controls in place, including portfolio selection, reporting, and decision-making (Muller, Martinsuo, & Blomquist, 2008).

Organizational Culture

Beyond having PPM processes and procedures, the effectiveness of PPM depends on the execution of those processes and procedures. Typically, successful execution depends on the behavioral norms of people within the organization. These behavioral norms are the products of the organizational culture (Schein, 1990). The evidence shows that all five companies participating in this study have different organizational cultures as a result of their different business environments. However, there are common elements of culture across these organizations: teamwork, collaboration, integrity, quality of information, and communication.

It is evident that the effectiveness of PPM depends greatly on teamwork and integrity that should be adopted in all levels of PPM practices. This is especially true during project selection and prioritization. At company *Delta*, for example, the PC consists of senior level managers representing various functions, including the businesses. With the sole authority in making funding decisions, the PC must work as a team to fund the projects that are aligned with *Delta*'s strategy. Lack of teamwork may result in funding decisions that benefit only particular functions or businesses instead of the company overall. Teamwork and collaboration are also important ingredients for project success. Making appropriate portfolio decisions also relies on communication and quality of information. This includes the information necessary for making funding decisions and information regarding project status for making proper go/ kill decisions. At company *Alpha*, for example, the Network

PMO executive greatly emphasizes communication both verti-cally and horizontally. Besides communications based on the chain of command, the executive emphasizes peer-to-peer com-munication to disseminate information.

The impact of organizational culture on effectiveness is not new to the literature. However, the impact of organizational cul-ture on PPM effectiveness has not been thoroughly investigated. This finding supports the literature on organizational culture and effectiveness (Gregory, Harris, Armenakis, & Shook, 2009). The finding also goes along the same lines as the results of the studies on organizational culture and team effectiveness, which found that a group-oriented culture that supports commitment, communication, and teamwork has a positive effect on team ef-fectiveness (Campany, Dubinsky, Druskat, Mangino, & Flynn, 2007; Denison et al., 1996; Jassawalla & Sashittal, 2000; Jha & Iyer, 2007; Moenaert, Caeldries, Lievens, & Wauters, 2000).

Committed, Active, and Competent Participants

Committed, active, and competent participants have direct impact on PPM effectiveness. The participants include the senior executives, PPM managers, PMO managers, committee members, middle managers, and project managers.

In *Alpha*'s case, the president and senior executives are very committed to project management and PPM. The president is hands-on and pays close attention to the status of strategically important projects. The president reviews the project portfo-lio monthly, which also requires senior executives to have a monthly review of projects in their function. In particular, it is a request from the president that the project teams must report the impact of project performance on the revenue. The Network PMO executive and PMO directors are also committed to proj-ect management. The executive calls a weekly meeting to dis-cuss human resource and project issues that need immediate attention. The PMO directors also have a weekly meeting with the project managers in their directorate. In company *Beta*, senior executives are the active participants of project prioritization and project governance. The PMO manager takes an active role in managing conflicts across projects and is on top of project management issues. The PMO manager has two separate weekly meetings with the project managers to (1) discuss resource conflict in the upcoming two weeks and (2) go over the dashboard, milestones, and processes.

Similar to other organizations, *Delta* also has committed, active, and competent PPM participants. As a chair of PC and GC, the PPMO director takes an active role in managing the corporate project portfolio. The success of the committees depends greatly on the commitment of the committee members. The PC is comprised of senior-level managers representing various functions, including the businesses. The PC meets monthly to make funding and go/kill decisions. The PC also meets quarterly to perform portfolio balancing. The GC has 11 members who meet every week to review project proposals, the viability of project plans, project execution, risks, and plan deviations in order to make the recommendations to the PC. The CEO and senior executives (management committee) at *Delta* do not involve themselves in portfolio decisions. However, they set the company's strategic direction that influences the activities of the PC. The management committee receives reports from the PC regarding the status of the portfolio.

Gamma's CIO (Chief Information Officer) takes an active role in its PPM process. The CIO and the CAO (Chief Administrative Officer) are the co-chairs of the committee that are responsible for project selection and governance. Presidents of businesses, as well as CFOs and COOs, are parts of the committee. The CIO also chairs additional committees in the PPM process, including a monthly project review. In *Lambda*'s case, the SC&T director is a visionary and a hands-on leader. The director takes an active role in project selection and governance. The SC&T director is the chair of the project review committee. In sum, it is evident in all cases that committed, active, and competent participants are significant to PPM effectiveness. This finding supports several propositions suggested by other researchers with regards to role of the portfolio manager and management involvement (Jonas, 2010).

In conclusion, the results from this study suggest five factors that contribute to PPM effectiveness. They are the formal strategic planning and capital budgeting; organizational entities responsible for project and portfolio management and their organizational placement; frameworks and processes for project portfolio management and information systems support; organizational culture; and committed, active, and competent participants (see Figure 1).

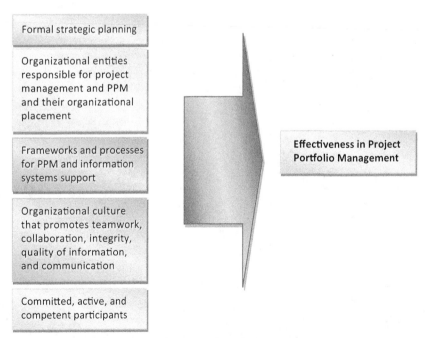

Figure 1: Factors contributing to PPM effectiveness.

Chapter 6

Measuring Project Portfolio Management Effectiveness

PPM effectiveness should be measured using outcome measurements and process measurements. The outcome measurements assess PPM effectiveness based on the accomplishment of the portfolio outcomes. While measuring the ultimate outcomes of the portfolio in terms of realized benefits is necessary, the intermediate measurement to assess projected benefits and to evaluate whether or not the portfolio is managed according to its goals is also important. With the expectation that effective PPM process should lead to the accomplishment of portfolio outcomes, it is necessary that process measurements be developed to evaluate the efficacy of the processes and to evaluate whether or not the process will generate the desired outcomes.

Measuring PPM Effectiveness in the Context of Each Organization

As indicated in the previous chapter, the research evidence suggests that, to a certain extent, PPM has been practiced in the five organizations we studied, but none of them explicitly defines effectiveness in project portfolio management. Also, even though these organizations have attempted to assess their PPM, their measurements need to be further developed.

In *Alpha's* case, senior executives are interested in the benefits generated by the projects, especially the monetary benefits, such as revenue. Besides those benefits, *Alpha's* executives also pay attention to the effectiveness of the process. They assess whether or not projects go through the process in a reasonable period of time. Some measurements that they have implemented include Time-in-Stage, Time-to-Launch, and Time-in-Revision. Committed launch date achievement is another measurement implemented by *Alpha*. For *Beta*, the Development PMO emphasizes process effectiveness, especially the use of resources. *Beta* sees the benefits of PPM as a way to promote project visibility and the transparency of resource allocation. The ability to hit the baseline plan is another measurement of effectiveness at *Beta*. For *Delta*, PPM is assessed from two perspectives. The project management perspective emphasizes the predictability of project delivery, in terms of meeting budget, schedule, and scope expectation. From the portfolio management perspective, *Delta* evaluates their PPM by assessing the process outcomes such as spending budget, portfolio balance, and risk mitigation. In addition, *Delta* has put forth some efforts to measure project benefits, including average first benefit dollar and percentage of benefit realized. At *Gamma*, management pays attention to the effectiveness of project execution in terms of the project visibility and project delivery. As a government center, *Lambda* emphasizes process effectiveness in terms of predictability of project delivery. Besides focusing on the use of funds (obligation of money), senior management put more attention to technology transition. They assess whether or not the SC&T projects are transferable to development and operations in responding to the war fighter needs.

Toward a Measurement of PPM Effectiveness

Based on what we have learned from the case studies and our definition of PPM effectiveness, we propose a measurement of PPM effectiveness in this section. From our definition, PPM effectiveness is *"The organizational capability to (1) form and govern a project portfolio such that the portfolio aligns with the organization's strategic direction, addresses risks and opportunities, and is adaptive to the internal and external changes, in order to provide short and long-term value or benefits to the organization, and (2) to manage projects in the portfolio to promote transparency, process consistency, visibility and predictability of projects in the portfolio, and to promote integrity, cohesion, and the morale of the project community."* This effectiveness definition suggests that PPM effectiveness can be assessed using outcome measurements and process measurements.

Outcome Measurements

The effectiveness of PPM should be measured based on the accomplishment of portfolio outcomes. Outcome measurements can be categorized into ultimate outcome measurements and intermediate outcome measurements.

Ultimate outcome measurements assess the short and long-term value of the portfolio to the organization. We learned from the case study that company *Delta* has a plan to measure the short and long-term value of their portfolio. One way to measure the value of the portfolio is to assess the financial benefits generated by projects in the portfolio. These financial benefits can be measured in terms of revenue or cost saving, for example, as the "realized benefits" after the completion of the projects. To do so, management can create actual benefit realization metrics to measure such benefits over time versus planned. Besides realizing the benefits generated by the precedent portfolio and validating the decisions previously made, the information from these metrics can educate individuals such that appropriate decisions can be made when managing the current portfolio. In many cases, the project value cannot be measured directly in terms of financial benefits (Patanakul & Shenhar, 2010). For those projects, their benefits must be clearly articulated during project initiation and must be monitored as part of portfolio governance. In some cases, those benefits may be quantifiable. Such benefits as operational efficiency, for example, are measured in terms of time savings or customer complaints. Some surrogate measurements can also be used to monitor the benefits of these projects. For example, in *Lambda*'s case, the SC&T director pays attention to the value of the SC&T portfolio by using technology transition as a surrogate measurement. If the benefits are not quantifiable, it is also possible to develop some rating scales to assess the benefits of the projects. These quantifiable benefits and rating scales can also be used in the actual benefit realization metrics.

While the ultimate outcome measurements are used to assess the short and long-term value of the portfolio once the projects are completed, *intermediate outcome measurements* can be developed to assess the projected benefits during project execution, with the expectation that the realized benefits will be attained. Examples of intermediate outcome measurement are the assessment of projected revenue or projected cost savings. In *Alpha*'s case, senior executives focus on revenue generated by the network project portfolio. They closely monitor the projected revenue when performing portfolio governance. Besides the projected benefits, another set of measurements can be developed to assess the intermediate outcomes of PPM in terms of the attainment of PPM goals. These measurements can be used to evaluate whether or not the portfolio aligns with the organization's strategic direction, addresses risks and opportunities, and is adaptive to the internal and external changes.

The expectation is that the achievement of PPM goals will lead to the achievement of the realized benefits. To assess whether or not the portfolio aligns with the organization's strategic direction, metrics can be developed to assess the number of projects in the portfolio that contribute to each strategic direction. The contribution of the portfolio to the strategic direction can also be assessed in terms of spending budget (Cooper et al., 2001). Similar metrics can be created to assess whether or not the portfolio addresses risks and opportunities. For example, metrics can be developed to assess the degree of technological risks and market risks of each project in the portfolio. In terms of the adaptability of the portfolio to the internal and external changes, some scenario analyses can be performed to assess the sensitivity of the portfolio to the changes in strategic priority and competitive environments, for example. The low degree of sensitivity indicates the high level of adaptability or tolerance to changes. At the aggregated level, the results from these assessments should indicate the degree of accomplishment of PPM goals.

Process Measurements

Besides the outcome measurements, the effectiveness of PPM should be measured based on the effectiveness of PPM processes. The expectation is that an effective process should lead to the accomplishment of the portfolio outcomes. We learned from many cases that the use of processes is to help promote the predictability of project delivery. So, as part of process measurement, the predictability of project delivery should be assessed. One way to do so is to measure the percentage accomplishment of projects in the portfolio in terms of time, cost, and scope. The results from this assessment should indicate the effectiveness of the process and the potential achievement of the expected benefits from the portfolio.

Process measurements should also be developed to assess the level of transparency in decision making, the consistency in the use of processes, the efficacy of the processes, the availability of information systems support, the visibility of projects to senior management, and the level of integrity, cohesion, and morale of the project community. These items can be measured quantitatively and qualitatively. The efficacy of the processes can be quantitatively measured based on time (e.g., the actual time that a project needs to go through various stages vs. plan, number of iterations at each stage, and number of resource conflicts). Besides the quantitative measurement, a questionnaire with rating scales can be developed to assess these items qualitatively. Even though these measurements are subjective in nature, the results from these measurements should indicate the overall process effectiveness, which can lead to the delivery of successful portfolio outcomes. From the case study, several organizations have attempted to assess the effectiveness of the process. *Delta* uses a questionnaire to assess such effectiveness. On the other hand, *Gamma*'s CIO, by observation, has recognized that the levels of process consistency and project visibility have increased.

Besides asking the informants to directly assess processes, a questionnaire should be designed to ask questions regarding work climate, especially one that impacts PPM effectiveness (refer to the key factors in Chapter 5). For example, questions can be designed to assess the level of understanding of an organization's strategic direction, the level of communication both vertically and horizontally, the level of commitment both from top management and project community, the level of teamwork and collaboration, and the quality of information. The results from these assessments provide valuable information as the lead indicator of the accomplishment of PPM effectiveness.

In conclusion, we propose that the PPM effectiveness should be measured using outcome measurements and process measurements (see Table 2). The outcome measurements assess PPM

Table 2: Examples of measurements of PPM effectiveness.

Measurement category		Example
Outcome measurements	**Ultimate outcome measurements**	Realized benefits	Revenue and cost saving, operating efficiency (time saving, customer complaints), surrogate measurements, and a questionnaire with rating scales (for non-quantifiable items)
	Intermediate outcome measurements	Projected benefits	Projected revenue or cost saving, and a questionnaire with rating scales
		PPM goals attainment: Portfolio alignment, addressing risk and opportunity, adaptability to the internal and external changes	Number of projects contributing to each strategic direction, spending budget, portfolio risk metrics, scenario analysis, and degree of accomplishment using a questionnaire with rating scales

(continued)

Table 2: *Continued*

Measurement category		Example
	Predictability of project delivery	Percentage accomplishment in terms of time, cost, and scope
Process measurements	Process goals: Transparency of decision making, visibility of projects, efficacy of processes, availability of information, and morale of project community	Time-in-stage, number of iterations, number of re-source conflicts, and degree of accomplishment using a questionnaire with rating scales
	Work climate: Level of understanding of strategic direction, communication, commitment, teamwork and collaboration, quality of information	Degree of agreement using a questionnaire with rating scales

effectiveness based on the accomplishment of the portfolio out-comes. While measuring the ultimate outcomes of the portfolio in terms of realized benefits is necessary, the intermediate mea-surement to assess projected benefits and to evaluate whether or not the portfolio is managed according to its goals are also important. With the expectation that an effective PPM process should lead to the accomplishment of the portfolio outcomes, it is necessary that process measurements be developed to evaluate the efficacy of the processes and to evaluate whether or not the process will generate the desirable outcomes.

Chapter 7

Contributions and Implications

This qualitative study was conducted to investigate the PPM practices of organizations in order to propose a definition of PPM effectiveness, identify key factors impacting PPM effectiveness, and propose measurements of PPM effectiveness. From this study, PPM effectiveness is *the organizational capability to (1) form and govern a project portfolio such that the portfolio aligns with the organization's strategic direction, addresses risks and opportunities, and is adaptive to the internal and external changes in order to provides short and long-term value or benefits to the organization, and (2) to manage projects in the portfolio to promote transparency, process consistency, visibility and predictability of projects in the portfolio, and to promote integrity, cohesion, and the morale of the project community.* The research findings also suggest keys factors impacting PPM effectiveness, which include (1) the formal strategic planning and capital budgeting process, (2) organizational entities responsible for project and portfolio management and their organizational placement, (3) frameworks and processes for project portfolio management and information systems support, (4) organizational culture, and (5) committed, active, and competent participants. In terms of measurement, PPM effectiveness should be measured using (1) outcome measurements and (2) process measurements. The outcome measurements assess

PPM effectiveness based on the accomplishment of the portfolio outcomes. The process measurements help evaluate the efficacy of the processes and evaluate whether or not the process may generate desirable outcomes.

The results of this study contribute to the theory and practice of project portfolio management. In terms of the theoretical contribution, first, this research proposes an empirically grounded definition of PPM effectiveness that serves as a platform for future studies on PPM effectiveness. Future studies can be conducted to investigate the linkage between PPM effectiveness and organizational effectiveness and the linkage between PPM effectiveness and project management effectiveness or team effectiveness. These studies should promote a better understanding of organizational effectiveness, especially in the context of a project-oriented organization. In addition, to further improve the definition of PPM effectiveness, future research can be conducted to validate and fine-tune this definition to different settings. Second, this study identifies key factors impacting PPM effectiveness. Researchers can use these findings as a basis for conducting more focused studies to further understand how these factors impact PPM effectiveness. Future studies can be conducted to investigate the relationships among these factors and their impact on PPM effectiveness. This includes studies on mediating and moderating relationships among these factors. Third, this study proposes measurements of PPM effectiveness. These measurements can be used to assess PPM effectiveness in future sample studies.

For practitioners, the findings of this study provide several managerial implications. First, the study reveals

PPM practices of five organizations. These organizations have different goals toward the implementation of PPM, and therefore, represent different levels of PPM maturity. Practitioners can use this information as a benchmark for development and improvement of their PPM practices. Second, the study proposes a definition of PPM effectiveness, derived from the research evidence and literature review. By understanding what PPM effectiveness is, practitioners should be able to develop and implement a PPM approach that will enhance the effectiveness. While an overall definition of PPM effectiveness was proposed in this study, practitioners should contingently adopt this definition. Within one organization, different functions may have different responsibilities for PPM. Those functions should focus on certain elements of PPM effectiveness that are relevant to their responsibilities. As discussed in this study, the Development PMO of *Beta* was not responsible for project selection and prioritization. Their main responsibility was the successful delivery of projects in the portfolio. While overall PPM effectiveness should be achieved, the PPM effectiveness in the context of the Development PMO should be perceived in terms of resource allocation, project success, and integrity, cohesion, morale, and learning of the project management community. Third, since the study reveals key factors impacting PPM effectiveness, it gives practitioners guidelines on what conditions they should create to promote PPM effectiveness. Fourth, the measurements of PPM effectiveness proposed in this study should provide practitioners with a basis for developing appropriate measurements contingent to their organization and PPM practice.

References

Archer, N. P., & Ghasemzadeh, F. (1999). An integrated framework for project portfolio selection. *International Journal of Project Management, 17*(4), 207–216.

Bard, J. F., Balachandra, R., Kaufmann, P. E. (1988). An interactive approach to R&D project selection and termination. *IEEE Transactions on Engineering Management, 35*(3), 139.

Blomquist, T., & R. Muller, R. (2006). Practices, roles, and responsibilities of middle managers in program and portfolio management. *Project Management Journal, 37*(1), 52–66.

Brudney, J. L., & Englund, R. E. (1982). Urban policy making and subjective science evaluations: Are they compatible? *Public Administration Review, 42*(2), 127–135.

Cameron, K., & D. A. Whetten, D. A. (1983). *Organizational effectiveness: A comparison of multiple models.* New York: Academic Press.

Cameron, K. S. (1979). Evaluating organizational effectiveness in organized anarchies. Academy of Management Meeting, Atlanta, GA.

Campany, N., Dubinsky, R., Druskat, V., Mangino, M., & Flynn, E. (2007). What makes good teams work better: Research-based strategies that distinguish top-performing cross-functional drug development teams. *Organization Development Journal, 25*(2), 179.

Campbell, J. P. (1977). On the nature of organizational effectiveness. In P. S. Goodman & J. M. Pennings (eds.), *New perspectives on organizational effectiveness (pp. 13–55).* San Francisco: Jossey-Bass.

Chandler, A. D. (1962). *Strategy and structure.* Cambridge, MA: MIT Press.

Chiu, L., & Gear, T. E. (1979). An application and case history of a dynamic R&D portfolio selection model. *IEEE Transactions on Engineering Management, 26*(1), 2.

Cohen, S. G., Ledford, G.E., & Spreitzer, G. M. (1996). A predictive model of self-managing work team effectiveness. *Human Relations, 49*(5), 643–676.

Cooper, R. G., Edgett S. J., & Kleinschmidt, E. J. (2001). *Portfolio management for new products.* New York, NY: Basic Books.

Cooper, R. G., Edgett S. J., & Kleinschmidt, E. J. (2002). Optimizing the stage-gate process: What best-practice companies do-II. *Research Technology Management, 45*(6), 43–49.

Denison, D. R., Hart, S. L., & Kahn, J. A. (1996). From chimneys to cross-functional teams: Developing and validating a diagnostic model. *Academy of Management Journal, 39*(4), 1005–1023.

Dickinson, M. W., Thornton, A. C., Graves, S. (2001). Technology portfolio management: Optimizing interdependent projects over multiple time periods. *IEEE Transactions on Engineering Management, 48*(4), 518–527.

Eisenhardt, K. M. (1989). Building theories from case study research. *Academy of Management Review, 14,* 532–550.

Elmes, M., & Wilemon, D. (1988). Organizational culture and project leader effectiveness. *Project Management Journal, 19*(4), 54–63.

Golabi, K. (1987). Selecting a group of dissimilar projects for funding. *IEEE Transactions on Engineering Management, EM34*(3), 138.

Gregory, B. T., Harris, S. G., Armenakis, A. A., & Shook, C. L. (2009). Organizational culture and effectiveness: A study of values, attitudes, and organizational outcomes. *Journal of Business Research, 62*(7), 673.

Jassawalla, A. R., & Sashittal, H. C. (2000). Strategies of effective new product team leaders. *California Management Review, 42*(2), 34–51.

Jha, K. N., & Iyer, K. C. (2007). Commitment, coordination, competence and the iron triangle. *International Journal of Project Management, 25*(5), 527.

Jonas, D. (2010). Empowering project portfolio managers: How management involvement impacts project portfolio management performance. *International Journal of Project Management, 28*(8), 818–831.

Kendall, G. I., & Rollins, S. C. (2003). *Advanced project portfolio management and the PMO: Multiplying ROI at warp speed.* Boca Raton, FL: J. Ross Publishing.

Khorramshahgol, R., & Gousty, Y. (1986). Delphic goal programming (DGP): A multi-objective cost/benefit approach to R&D portfolio analysis. *IEEE Transactions on Engineering Management, EM33*(3), 172.

Kira, D. S., Kusy, M. I., Murray, D. H., & Goranson, B. J. (1990). A specific decision support system (SDSS) to develop an optimal project portfolio mix under uncertainty. *IEEE Transactions on Engineering Management, 37*(3), 213.

Lewin, A. Y., & Minton, J. W. (1986). Determining organizational effectiveness: Another look, and an agenda for research. *Management Science, 32*(5), 514–538.

Likert, R. (1961). *New patterns of management.* New York: McGraw-Hill.

Madey, G. R., & Dean, B. V. (1985). Straetgic planning for investment in R&D using decision analysis and mathematical programming. *IEEE Transactions on Engineering Management, EM32*(2), 84.

Martinsuo, M., & Lehtonen, P. (2007). Role of single-project management in achieving portfolio management efficiency. *International Journal of Project Management, 25*(1), 56.

Mathieu, J., Maynard, M. T., Rapp, T., & Gilson, L. (2008). Team effectiveness 1997–2007: A review of recent advancements and a glimpse into the future. *Journal of Management, 34*(3), 410–476.

Mayo, E. (1933). *The human problems of an industrial civilization.* New York: Macmillan.

McGrath, J. E. (1964). *Social psychology: A brief introduction.* New York: Holt, Rinehart & Winston.

McGregor, D. (1960). *The human side of enterprise.* New York: McGraw-Hill.

Miles, M., & Huberman, A. (1980). *Qualitative data analysis: An expanded sourcebook*. London: Sage Publications.

Moenaert, R. K., F. Caeldries, et al. (2000). Communication flows in international product innovation teams. *Journal of Product Innovation Management, 17,* 360–377.

Morrison, J., & Brown, C. (2004). Project managment effectiveness as a constrcut: A conceptual study. *South African Journal of Business and Management, 35*(4), 73–94.

Muller, R., M. Martinsuo, et al. (2008). Project portfolio control and portfolio management performance in different contexts. *Project Management Journal, 29*(3), 28.

Patanakul, P., & Shenhar, A. J. (2010). Exploring the concept of value creation in program planning and systems engineering. *Systems Engineering, 13*(4), 340–352.

Pennings, J. M., & Goodman, P. S. (1977). Toward a workable framework. In P. S. Goodman & J. M. Pennings (eds.), *New perspectives on organizational effectiveness (pp. 146–184)*. San Francisco: Jossey-Bass.

Phelan, T. M. (2004). The impact of effectiveness and efficiency on project success. School of Technology Management, Stevens Institute of Technology, Hoboken. Doctoral of Philosophy.

PMI (2006). *The standard for portfolio management*. Newtown Square, PA: Project Management Institute.

PMI (2008). *The standard for portfolio management*—second edition. Newtown Square, PA, Project Management Institute.

Quinn, R. E., & Rohrbaugh, J. (1983). A spatial model of effectiveness criteria: Towards a competing values approach to organizational analysis. *Management Science, 29,* 363–377.

Rad, P. F., & Levin, G. (2005). A formalized model for managing a portfolio of internal projects. *AACE International Transactions, PM41.*

Rajegopal, S., P. McGuin, et al. (2007). *Project portfolio management.* New York, NY: Palgrave Macmillan.

Schein, E. (1990). Organizational culture. *American Psychologist, 45*(2), 109–119.

Scott, R. W. (1977). Effectiveness of organizational effectiveness studies. In P. S. Goodman & J. M. Pennings (eds.), *New perspectives on organizational effectiveness (pp. 63–95)*. San Francisco: Jossey-Bass.

Seashore, S. E. (1979). Assessing organizational effectiveness with reference to member needs. Academy of Management Meeting, Atlanta, GA.

Spharim, I., & Szakonyi, R. (1984). A simple method for evaluation and selection of R&D proposals for a competitive grant fund. *IEEE Transactions on Engineering Management, EM31*(4), 184.

Stummer, C., & Heidenberger, K. (2003). Interactive R&D portfolio analysis with project interdependencies and time profiles of multiple objectives. *IEEE Transactions on Engineering Management, 50*(2), 175–183.

Taylor, F. W. (1911). *The principles of scientific management*. New York: Harper & Row.

Yin, R. (1984). Case study research: Design and methods. Beverly Hills, CA, Sage Publications.

About the Authors

Dr. Peerasit Patanakul is an associate professor at The Pennsylvania State University, Erie. Prior to joining PSU, he was an assistant professor at Stevens Institute of Technology. Dr. Patanakul's current research interests include project portfolio management and multiple project management, strategic and value-focused project management, and management of large-scale government projects. His works have been published in, for example, *IEEE Transactions on Engineering Management, Journal of Product Innovation Management, Journal of Engineering and Technology Management, International Journal of Project Management, Project Management Journal, Journal of High Technology Management Research, and Journal of General Management*. He is a co-author of a book entitled *"Case Studies in Project, Program, and Organizational Project Management"* (Wiley, 2010). Dr. Patanakul received his B.E. from Chulalongkorn University, Thailand; and MS and PhD degrees from Portland State University, USA.

Audrey Curtis holds a PhD in experimental psychology. While conducting this research she was the executive director of the Graduate Programs in Project Management and Telecommunications Management, and was a distinguished professor in the Howe School of Technology Management at Stevens Institute of Technology. She is now retired. Prior to joining Stevens, Dr. Curtis was the chief technology officer at eLink Communications. She was vice president of technology strategy and product alignment at Concert, the joint venture between AT&T and British Telecom, and had a 26-year career at Bell Labs and AT&T Labs, holding a variety of executive and technical managerial positions in research and development, systems engineering, and technology transfer.

 Brian Koppel, PMP currently manages a PMO for a Fortune 500 company, while pursuing his PhD in technology management at Stevens Institute of Technology. He holds an MBA in finance and information systems from New York University. Brian has over 15 years of experience in project and program management and PMO in the financial services and healthcare industries. His research interests include project portfolio management and the program management office.